# Happiness Loves Company
# *Too*

Anthony Jameyson

# Happiness Loves Company
## *Too*

Happiness Loves Company Too

Published in 2022 by

Seven Door Multimedia, LLC

2000 Powers Ferry Rd.

Ste 2116

Marietta, GA 30067

Library of Congress Cataloging-in-Publications-Data

Unless otherwise indicated, Scripture quotations are from the Amplified or King James Version of the Holy Bible. All rights reserved.

Printed in the United States of America

10 9 8 7 6 5 4 3 2 1

# Acknowledgements

Let me start by saying that I am profoundly grateful that God would give me wisdom to turn my sadness into happiness.

I want to thank all of my family and friends who trust me to share positive thoughts that will add greater value to life. Thank you, to my mentors, for taking time to help build, strengthen, and encourage me when I was at my lowest. I honestly believe that we sometimes don't understand all we encounter in life, but there are people who are there to help guide us along the way. Last, I want to give a special thanks to DiShan Washington, and her team at Seven Door Multimedia, for the professionalism put into this book.

My life definitely has proved to me that happiness is a choice. The key is to obtain happiness for you. Never depend on anyone to make you happy, in fact, they should only add to the happiness you have already discovered for yourself. It is often said that misery loves company. Well, happiness is a destination of the heart, and you must have a desire to travel there too.

# Chapter One

We have all heard the phrase that misery loves company. In fact, many of us have had our own experiences when it comes to having friends that were in a miserable head space. It's definitely not a good feeling at all, especially when we end up becoming just like them.

Being miserable is draining and whether we know it or not, it takes more energy to be miserable than it does to be happy. To be miserable, you have to intentionally feel down, talk down, look down and continually be upset. Many of us have been hurt by situations we never thought would force us into a place of misery. But just because some tough things have happened, you do not have to stay where those tough things dropped you off.

In order to tackle misery and embrace happiness, you must do it head on, and learn to control your thoughts. If you are like most, you've at some point underestimated the power of your thoughts. Which means you are losing 90% of what you could potentially achieve in your life.

But don't worry, you're not alone. In our society, unfortunately, human thoughts are often relegated to the level of fantasy and extravagance, and it's for this reason, only a small percentage are really happy and content with their lives.

Our thoughts create our emotions, and our emotions create our state of mind. When events happen, we react according to the state of mind we are in at that moment; in fact, our behavior in life is the result of the state we're in. Whatever we do in our life, or whatever happen to us in our life, it's what we thought about that situation, event, person, circumstance etc. that is important—it all starts from there, it creates how we feel.

Our life is the result of our feelings, we make decisions based on how we feel, we react to situations based on how we feel.

Does it make sense?

If we are angry and something happens, we react in a certain way, but if we are happy we might react in a different way.

So, if most of the time we think of something negative, we will create a negative emotion and, accordingly, a negative state of mind. A negative state of mind means periods or moments of unhappiness. Of course, the opposite is also true if we spend more time with positive thoughts; we create more positive emotions and consequently a positive mental state that result in happiness. So, we have the power to decide whether we want to be happy, just by choosing our thoughts.

Positive thinking can sound simple, but often, not easy. Our life is made of habits and even Buddha once said: "We are what we think." Therefore, it's especially important to constantly choose positive way of thinking and make an optimistic attitude your habit or second nature.

Let me share with you some advantages of being a positive, happy person:

**1) Positive mind attracts positive events.**

First, if we decide to become positive, we can make the so called "law of attraction" work in our favor. The main principle of the law of attraction is that "like attracts like." If you will make positive thinking your habitual way of seeing life, imagine how many great things you can attract into your life. Thus, the title of this book: Happiness Loves Company Too!

## 2) Great and harmonious relationships.

When you choose a positive attitude, you will start to notice a lot of positive qualities in people and ignore their faults, and then, you will start to create more meaningful friendships and great relationships. This type of attitude will create an incredibly good and positive atmosphere around you.

## 3) Health

Positive thinking is beneficial for your health. Several scientific studies have shown that people with a good, positive "vibe" are less likely to suffer from depression and they get ill more rarely than the negative thinkers. In many cases, bad thoughts are the main cause of diseases, and even the word "disease" means that the person is not at ease. Thus, if you change your thoughts, you will change your life. That's why taking care of our thoughts is taking care of our health.

## 4) Key of success

Positive people are more likely to be successful than the negative ones. When you implement positive thinking into your life, you will notice that success becomes easier and is not as tough and difficult as many people think.

## 5) No more stress.

The main cause of stress is worry and negative thoughts. If we think about it, we can understand that stress never solves problems, but on the contrary, it can leave us helpless. Positive people overcome stress more easily. When you start to increase the quantity of good and positive thoughts, stress will gradually leave your life.

**6) Positive thinking and optimistic attitude will turn all your problems into opportunities.**

Negativity can blind people's mind. If you turn your thoughts from the negative ones into positive, your eyes will be opened and you will see the bottle half full, instead of half empty. You will start to notice solutions and will understand that every problem is an opportunity to gain experience. With that said, all problems can be solved.

**7) You will notice the abundance of good things in your life.**

Sometime people live their life without knowing how blessed they really are, they take things for granted and forget to be thankful. As I mentioned earlier, there are certain laws in life, one of them says: "like attracts like" and another is: "you will reap what you sow." When people live their lives complaining, and mourning about their destiny, without appreciating the things that they already have, they risk losing even this. Appreciation and gratitude, on the contrary, can bring more good things to be thankful for into their life. So, let's be thankful and let's count our blessings.

**8) Boost of motivation.**

Positive attitude will boost your motivation and you will start to achieve your goals quicker and easier. To have strong motivation is the same as to have "wings" that enable you to fly anywhere.

**9) Beauty will shine from within.**

Positive thinking will make you look more beautiful. It happens naturally: smiling, friendly and happy people are, somehow, extremely attractive. Your inner beauty will shine and will become visible on the outside, as well.

"People tend to have a cognitive bias toward their failures, and toward negativity," says Matthew Della Porta, a positive psychologist and organizational consultant. Her point is, our brains are more likely to seek out negative information and store it more quickly to memory.

Of course, that bias is not always bad. Acknowledging problems and facing failures can lead us to better solutions. But too often, we go overboard, and beat ourselves up for our failures or let ourselves dwell in the negative.

By consciously increasing our focus on the positive, we start to even the balance. We find a happy medium where we can address failures and challenges without letting them get us down, leaving us more motivated, productive, and likely to succeed.

Here are three ways you can train your brain to stay positive.

## 1. Express gratitude.

Negative events loom large unless you consciously balance them out. When you're faced with challenges, it's important to take inventory of what's going well. Thinking about the good in your life can help balance that bias, which gives your brain the extra time it needs to register and remember a positive event.

To help your brain store positive events, reflect on what you're grateful for and why. Write down your blessings, such as the opportunity to pursue a career you love or a family that supports you or a relationship that might be going well. If you need a daily habit, then keep a journal of good things that happened during the day.

## 2. Repeat positive affirmations.

As any politician or advertiser knows, the more often you hear a message, the more likely you are to believe it. The same goes for messages about who you are and of what you are capable. By repeating positive affirmations with conviction several times each morning, you are training your brain to believe them, and over time, you'll start to internalize them.

Choose two to three affirmations that represent your values and goals, such as, 'I can manage whatever comes my way,' 'There is plenty of time,' or 'I'm getting better every day.' The repetition will influence the way you interpret negative events, making you more resilient. If you're predisposed to negative thinking, this can be extremely effective.

### 3. Challenge negative thoughts.

Each time a negative thought arises, we choose how to respond. If left to our own devices, we tend to dwell. Our brains tend to focus on negative events, so they seem much bigger and more significant than they are. To combat that, start by imagining the thought as separate from yourself, as something you can observe and deconstruct. Get in the habit of distancing yourself instead of dwelling there.

Next, challenge negative thoughts that are self-deprecating. For example, if your new business or venture doesn't get the traction you hoped, you might think, "I'm a failure." That's untrue and unproductive. Instead, practice interpreting the same event differently. You might say, I worked hard but I didn't account for a drop in the market, so I'm disappointed, but now I'm going to try again with new information. That interpretation is truer and more initiative-taking. Over time, it'll become automatic and negative thoughts will be less likely to come up. No one does this naturally; you have to learn and practice.

Friends, simply put, this book was written to aid you in living your best life, and to do that, you must learn how to be happy no matter what state you find yourself in.

It is my hope that by the time you turn the last page, you will be one step closer to living the life you deserve with the kinds of relationships you're deserving of as well.

# Chapter Two

If one is going to be happy in their life, they must learn the art of patience. No one sails through life without docking on the shores of patience a time or two. Patience is an essential part of the bedrock of happiness because you must quickly understand that sometimes life doesn't always pan out the way we think it will, or the way we think it should. Having patience will allow you to accept those changes without having a pessimistic attitude about things you cannot control. If things are not going the way you want them to, instead of getting frustrated, you must learn to be patient. You need to see things and situations in a positive light to make your life happier. And to get that positivity, you need to be patient.

If you find any life situation challenging, or find it difficult to bear, try to re-frame that situation and try to see its positive side. To say patience is a virtue is an understatement. It's really more of a skill—one that can be learned and needs constant nurturing. Patience is the state of being that occurs between experience and reaction. Whether you're trying to be patient with yourself, others, or life, it always involves the experience of dealing with delays or obstacles.

By cultivating a practice of patience, you're able to let go of things outside your control and live with less stress, anxiety, and frustration. It's not an easy practice, but here are a few perspectives on how to cultivate patience to open up new possibilities.

When you look at what it means to have patience, you're talking about dealing with your own thoughts and emotions. As a spiritual being there is an unbounded, limitless presence within you that is constantly seeking expression. You think, act, and experience, and this should be the simplicity of life. Unfortunately, it's not that simple. Problems arise when what you think and do doesn't seem to produce immediate results. It's time to look inward and ask why you don't have patience with yourself. Ask yourself:

- What does it mean to be patient with myself?
- What benefits would I experience by being patient with myself?
- What can I do to become more patient with myself?

Remember that patience is the ability to not be troubled by life's changes, delays, or other undesirables. It's the ability to maintain stillness in the midst of disappointment.

Try to practice self-awareness in those moments where you feel the greatest need for patience.

- Pay attention to what arises in you
- Notice where you feel the stress
- Listen to your thoughts
- Take note of your emotions

A powerful benefit to practicing patience is that you cultivate the peace of mind to guide yourself out of these moments. Even the simple act of looking within at a time when you're feeling impatient can be healing.

Use awareness to maintain your calm. Tap into your stillness and preserve it. See these moments of self-reflection as opportunities to strengthen yourself in self-control and grace. I know you may be reading that thinking it is so much easier said than done. And I feel you. But, hey, change doesn't happen overnight anyway.

I began transforming from being pessimistic to optimistic because I became weary of getting the same results. I once believed that if I anticipated the worst, I could guard myself against disappointments. If I could survive the walls caving in around me, then that was the best I could expect. Focusing on nothing more than the less didn't amount to anything at all in my eyes because without even realizing it, this became my ceiling, and nothing went beyond that limit. Before reaching my breaking point, or shall I say awakening, I used to ask myself, *"How would things get better? What am I doing wrong?"* Then, it hit me like a ton of bricks. *"Anthony, you can't be more negative than you are positive."* So, I started to observe my words and actions towards other people. I became more aware of how I was perceived, my actions, my energy, my vibe, my attitude, and my outlook on life. More than anything else, I became sensitive towards self. I began to explore areas of my heart and character. And like a revolving door, a ton of bricks hit me a second time "Anthony, you can't be more negative than you are positive."

As I stated earlier, patience is particularly important because it should be a person's foundation or anchor. It takes time to understand how to apply the brakes on what we may perceive as urgent. If an individual press too early, he or she will feel the need to get caught up before it spins out of control. If a person applies too late, then he or she will over think the situation. Therefore, leaving him or her vulnerable to panic attacks. This trait is critical because it should be a person's foundation or anchor.

Cultivating patience with others is an entirely different challenge. Other people are always acting, thinking, and feeling in ways that are potentially disagreeable. Since everyone has a right to personal freedom, no one has the right to hinder others from their life or personal self-expression—no matter how much you'd like to sometimes. It's hard to simply live and let live. The problem with this is that you're constantly surrounded by other people and the ways you live your life will be different. The gift of living through patience, however, is that you become less reactionary. When others let you down or irritate you, be patient with them. Gently express love and stillness. Remember that they are growing—just like you—and that life is a process. Whatever issues you may have with another person are more than likely temporary and will undoubtedly change once you let go of your own agenda. What disturbs you presently about this person may change and in the next moment you may laugh with them or feel some other positive emotion. Regardless of what other people do or think, you have a choice in how you allow it to affect you. Your mind may jump to negative notions and reactions, your body may even register a response, but you are the source of it all. You can tap into your stillness, your peace. Remember this and from this have patience. You are one with the eternal. The things, people, and situations in your life change. Patience is an expression of this awareness and of love.

Once I implemented patience towards all aspects of my life, (time is a key factor), I noticed a considerable change with everything. Time not only reveals how good things come to those who wait but also by moving slowly, I can see the bigger picture and adjust accordingly. Therefore, this valuable lesson has helped me recognize when I become eager or anxious about something new, the understanding of how to apply the brakes kick in towards what I may perceive as urgent. Before my transformation, pressing too early was truly a lifestyle.

Recently, I went through a divorce, and the amount of patience it took to endure that was unbelievable. I had to accept my ex-wife's point of view, although wrong, and allow patience to kick in as we navigated through the process. I didn't get married to get divorced, but I also didn't get married to be unhappy. The patience to allow things to be what they're going to be is a skill, nonetheless, the moment you embrace it, peace and happiness will settle over you like dew in the morning.

Gaining patience can be transformative to your overall life experience. So much of life is about awareness, growth, and learning—these are the things that are always going on behind the scenes. When you want things to happen in your life, you can prolong the process by giving your attention and energy to the frustration you feel about waiting. The waiting is not the problem. It's how you deal with it, how you see it. Practicing patience shifts your attention away from the stress and frustration. Acting with patience is a way of telling life that you are in charge. You are in no hurry, there is no distress—only peace and confidence in your truth. This is an imperial trait—one of strength and majesty over your life's circumstances.

Practicing patience will help you dissipate stress and give you a choice about how you respond to disappointment and frustration. When you can stay calm, centered, and not act rashly out of frustration, all areas of your life will improve, and happiness will flow in abundance.

# Chapter Three

How do you see yourself?

Once a person learns how to hold to the reigns of patience, the next step is to have a positive image of oneself. It doesn't matter if anyone else thinks you're great, if you don't think it, then it doesn't matter. A lot of people could live a happier life if they had a healthy image of themselves. I've seen so many individuals filled with potential waste their lives away because although I saw it, them not seeing it, caused them to never tap into it. If you are ever going to have a healthy relationship, or marriage, you've got to first have a healthy view of yourself. Otherwise, you will find yourself being mistreated, misunderstood, and misrepresented. You'll also tolerate things you shouldn't from people who don't possess the same love for you that you have for them. Have you ever found yourself crossing over oceans for people who would never even jump a puddle for you? Part of the reason you do that is because you're yet to view yourself as worthy of receiving the same type of energy.

While many profess not to care what others think, we are, in the end, creatures who want and need to fit into a social universe. Humans are psychologically suited to interdependence. Social anxiety is really just an innate response to the threat of exclusion; feeling that we're not accepted by a group leaves us agitated and depressed.

The ability to intuit how people see us is what enables us to authentically connect to others and to reap the deep satisfaction that comes with those ties. We can never be a fly on the wall to our own personality dissections, watching as people pick us apart after meeting us. Hence, we are left to rely on the accuracy of what psychologists call our "meta perceptions"—the ideas we have about others' ideas about us.

For years, and presently, I get dressed from head to toe, step in front of the mirror to say, "man, don't I look good" and (pause with a smirk on my face) to reply, "yes, I do." But this is only on the outside. For you see, some of my past relationships, personal and professional, were either destroyed, damaged, or discarded because I was blind to the positive things each one possessed. Have you had relationships that ended that shouldn't have ended? No worries. Most people have. Positivity also allows you to spot the red flags of negative behavior. A large sector of people never learned about love or how to maintain a relationship or marriage. Most of us wing it and hope for the best. The positive outcome for me after divorce was that although I made mistakes in the areas of communication and understanding, (which is paramount), I was not too removed from the point that I couldn't improve. I examined the part I played. Always be accountable for your own actions of involvement.

Let me tell you; insecurities play a significant role in whether you'll be happy or unhappy. If you lack the confidence to step outside the box and try things, more than likely you'll never find the happiness that could change your life for the better.

Most everyone has something about them that they would like to change. There is an important difference between the garden variety, "It would be nice to advance in my career, or have better time management, or lose a few pounds"; and the more painful, "I am fundamentally not okay because of X, Y,

Z." Examples include the heavy person who believes they need to lose weight to alleviate a sense of inner "badness"; the student who believes if they do not receive the top score, they will be a total failure; the single person who worries that their unpaired status proves that they are not really lovable; the professional who believes that they will only "matter" when they've crossed a certain earning threshold, and the like. Although for some, the internal insecurities feel less obvious than the physical ones, they are no less powerful at shaping what we think we are worth. These beliefs about ourselves can influence the goals we reach for, as well as our ability to accept good things for ourselves when they come our way.

1. Ask yourself, "What is it that I value?" Another way to phrase this may be, "What qualities do I admire in others?" Even if we may envy someone's fancy

house or slim thighs, chances are, what we respect about them has a lot more to do with how they conduct themselves, what's important to them, and how we feel when we are with them. Is this person loveable? Kind? Loving? Helpful? These qualities are the ones we, too, possess, or would like to further develop in ourselves.

2. Practice (self) forgiveness. Often it feels safer to consciously focus on something external or material that seems "not good enough," and not on the things we wish we'd done differently. I always emphasize that making mistakes is a normal part of learning. No one walks right out of the womb – we first learn to sit up, crawl, and wobble - falling innumerable times – before we can walk, and run, and play. Acknowledge what you'd like to do differently now –

the only time period in which we can act to make things better.

3. Set goals that are discreet, measurable, and in accordance with what you value. Also, leave room for goals that are fun. Realizing you can accomplish the things you set out to do – even mundane things – is part of how we build self-esteem.

4. Ask yourself each day, "What am I grateful for?" Everyone – and I do mean everyone -- if they are willing -- can find at least one small thing each day for which they can be thankful. Even when things seem bad, we can be grateful for someone's kindness, for some part of our body that works (even if we are ill), for the sun shining, for the lessons we can learn even from the difficult people in our lives, etc.

5. Visualize yourself shedding the harsh, outdated ideas about yourself that you no longer need. They actually don't do any good. See yourself feeling as you'd like to feel, doing the things that are most meaningful to you.

People have a need for affection and being liked. But it's quite easy to make a mistake here and go about it the wrong way. Because while trying to get others to like you may seem like a simple and common solution, there are alternatives.

Here are six:

**1. Liking yourself gives you power and strength.**

If you go for trying to get people to like you you'll come off as needy and desperate a lot of the time. This is a bad position to put yourself in. Because liking and respecting yourself goes hand in hand with people liking and respecting you. If you bend to other people all the time then they may like what you do for them. But they may not like you on a deeper level because there is a weakness and lack of confidence and personal power there.

## 2. People like people who like themselves.

What is attractive to a friend, an employer, or a potential partner? To me, it seems like a lot of this boils down to people liking people who like themselves. Someone who likes him/herself is positive, confident, takes care of his/her health and opportunities.

## 3. More inner stability, much less of an emotional rollercoaster.

Getting compliments and being liked is wonderful. The problem is just that if you rely too much on validation from others then you let the outside world, other people, control how you feel. And that can be a real rollercoaster. Because if you really need the positive validation from people then it's hard to avoid listening to their negative input. Or you may feel bad when there is a temporary lack in the validation. So, what do you do? You let go of focusing on needing that input and replace it with focusing on validating and liking yourself instead.

**4. Life becomes more fun and relaxing.**

If you like yourself then it becomes natural to just be your best self and let people like the real you. Doing the opposite and trying to get people to like you leads to a lack of honesty in any kind of relationship and life becomes a lot like walking on eggshells while using different masks with different people. Remember, happiness likes company, too!

## 5. What you think and feel about yourself flows over.

The more you like yourself, the easier it becomes to like, help and be kind to other people. How much you like or do not like yourself flows over into your world. In other words, your happiness is contagious.

## 6. You minimize self-sabotage.

If you don't like yourself, if you deep down don't really think you deserve what you go after then you will tend to sabotage yourself. In subtle ways. You may get a gut feeling that this success is wrong and so you start doing stuff that screws things up. If you like yourself there will be a lot less self-made obstacles in your mind to overcome on your path to success.

Don't take yourself for granted or focus on the wrong things. Appreciate yourself.

What you do or don't do has a huge effect on how you view yourself and how much you like yourself. But what you focus on in your mind is also important. Because if you do good things but then focus on small faults or failures that won't help you.

So, make a habit of focusing on appreciating the good things about yourself. Take two minutes right now to think about positive things about you, or good things you have done, and accomplished. The more you do things like these, the more this kind of thinking will naturally pop up in your everyday life, too. By doing this, you are changing how you think about yourself and what you tend to focus on.

# Chapter Four

I have found that a lot of times people are unhappy because they won't tell the truth. What do I mean about that? Well, I'm glad you asked. Have you ever done something you really didn't want to do but you did it anyway? Or have you ever agreed to something with which you really didn't agree? Most of us have done both of those things regardless to how miserable it made us feel. So many people do this every day instead of learning how to be honest with themselves and others.

Honesty.

Let's delve a little deeper.

My friend, truth is a bitter pill to swallow when relating to oneself. We often have the toughest times acknowledging the things we need to be better at which lead to inner happiness. For example, many of you reading this book have a bad habit of thinking the worst before you think the best. Have you ever walked inside a room full of happy people and felt they didn't want you there or convinced yourself that you were not going to enjoy? Did you try to think of any reason(s) to leave or not participate? If you answered yes to any of those questions, chances are you allow your pessimistic inner voice to speak louder than your positive voice. That, my friends, in and of itself is a deception to yourself. This is dangerous because it's one thing to lie to others, but to tell yourself a lie in your own voice is much worse.

If you are going to be happy, you have to do what is best for you. You have to understand and own your truth. People will always be around with their different opinions but that shouldn't matter to you. You should be so in tune with your purpose that nothing and no one can pull you away from it.

Some people are good at influencing others to do what they want them to do. But, when you are on the journey to being happy, being around influencers who specialize in trying to impose their thoughts and belief systems on other people isn't healthy or ideal.

Being honest with yourself means seeing yourself clearly, of course, but what does *that* mean? It's genuinely challenging to come to an accurate self-perception. Our perceptions of ourselves are informed by the stories we have told ourselves about ourselves. Those stories can be wildly inaccurate, and unfortunately judgmental.

Have you ever examined your personal narrative? What stories do you tell yourself about yourself? Have you ever considered that some of those stories might not be true? Have you ever examined where the stories you tell yourself about yourself came from and continue to come from? You have to be careful not to allow people to control the narrative to your life—it's your life.

A few places where the stories of ourselves come from: things our parents said, things our teachers said; things our peers said; things people we dated said; things our spouses say or said; comparisons we make between who we think we are and what we think we should be; stories we have created and believed in order to protect our fragile egos (and many of these stories can be, oddly, self-hating stories). Given the intensity and number of stories that we have internalized about ourselves, how can we ever see ourselves clearly and finally be honest with ourselves?

Being honest with yourself is a daily, hourly, even by-the-minute practice. The practice is being conscious of what we're doing and asking ourselves why we're doing it. At any given moment, what story are you telling yourself? Especially in moments of difficulty, being honest with yourself means separating yourself from your personal narrative. Can you step back from the running story of your life that runs through your head?

To step away from the story, we must step into something/somewhere else. Being real — being truly honest with yourself — happens when we focus completely on something outside ourselves. When we become so immersed in something that our *idea* of who we are exits the premises, is when honesty with ourselves is possible.

Being honest with yourself is not so common as it turns out we are blatant liars. Just listen to that inner dialogue without filtering for once.

Your turning point will come when you get uncomfortably honest with yourself. It does not matter that I did not *do* anything about it for a little while. I had taken that first step. I had stopped lying and started telling the truth to myself – not to the outside world, forget them for a minute please – but to YOURSELF.

Do you know what it's like to have that inner dialogue with your ego, to give up the pursuit of the only thing that you thought would make you "successful" after all the years of investment and sacrifice? Not a pretty day, yet it liberates you from the sham and drudgery of lying to your beautiful soul. I say that's worth it.

This stuff is not easy but let me tell you a secret: Easy sucks. Easy is over-rated. Easy for the lazy part of you that you need to eradicate. Easy gives your soul a virus. Easy is the pits. Easy is the road to misery. You need to forget about easy versus hard and stop whining about it. Your job, after you get honest with yourself, is to ask how and start figuring it out one step at a time.

Honesty comes with other issues too. Honesty brings you face to face with some ugly resistance at first. I could not separate my identity from my dream; I am my dream, I am my career, I am my ministry. I am meant to go down this path. I am not meant to go down the path of uncertainty. Complete resistance. So, stop resisting. Yes, that's as simple as it is. I am not trying to be cute or clever. Just stop resisting. Have you even tried? Stop resisting and go with the flow of that honesty. You won't die, I promise!

There is a good side to honesty, and this might comfort you. Changing what you know to be the only "truth" to listen to your soul is terrifying, and that's all you want to focus on because your mind wants you to resist the change, but if you pay attention, in all that fear and commotion, you will feel a little peace.

In the end of your life, whoever you are, you won't care anymore anyway, and then you will be utterly honest with yourself. Why not start sooner and actually do something about the divine message of honesty?

Honesty liberates you from your rules. It lifts heavy ugly weight off your shoulders and in that weight, you also store some good stuff, that's OK. Let them come off. You stored your security and comfort and predictable days and weeks and schedules. Let them go. You told yourself that life is supposed to be this way – miserable at times so you can be happy at other times – and you married that theory in a match made in hell. Let that go, too.

In those honest dialogues when you are really scared, truly vulnerable, and even clueless in some ways, you will know that you are willing to start over if only it means to stop the lying – I know I did.

So, are you being honest with yourself? How honest – all the way?

What do you want in life?

What do you want to be, do, have?

And what, if anything, are you doing about it?

# Chapter Five

While most of us would agree on the importance of reciprocal relationships, we don't consciously think about this idea of reciprocity when it comes to friendships and romantic relationships.

Reciprocity is a mutual exchange of actions, goods, energy, time, emotion, etc. between two people. Reciprocity is similar to a game of tennis or ping pong. There's a rhythm or a flow of a back-and-forth exchange. When someone reciprocates our efforts, it can leave us feeling validated in our choices and friendship, energized to keep going in this friendship or relationship and give more, and leaves us with this overall sense that we are valued and appreciated.

Meaningful friendships as well as romantic relationships requires investment, and reciprocity can be the gauge of whether or not the investment is worth it.

Often when people are challenged to assess the reciprocity, or the "give and take" in their relationships, a common complaint is they feel guilty and greedy for exploring how their relationships benefit them. Assessing reciprocity is not about "tit for tat," it about taking an honest look at the dynamics in your relationships and assessing the investment on each side.

Where in the relationship do you feel fulfilled? Where you each get your needs met and fulfillment in the relationship may be entirely different, and that's common. However, if you're unable to identify exactly what you've invested in and where you typically get something out of the relationship, then this may be a friendship you may want to reconsider.

*-Do you receive emotional support from this person? Encouragement?*

*-Is she/he there at a moment's notice when you're in need? Or, has this person filled this role regularly in the past?*

*-Do you feel you can be completely honest with this person, even if it poses potential conflict?*

*-Does this person serve as inspiration? Either through words or action?*

*-Do you feel (more often than not) that this person has your best interest at heart?*

Realistically, reciprocity between two people may not always have a constant and even flow. Depending on people's life circumstances, they may not be able to give as much as they are receiving from you. They just had their first child, or they lost a parent, or they just went through a significant move. However, this is where the concept of investment comes in. Do you feel the two of you have invested enough in the relationship in the past that you have a strong enough foundation to be more of the giver during this time? The most important question to ask yourself in such a situation is, do you believe your friend would do the same for you? Would he/she sacrifice her needs and be the friend you need during this time? If your answer is yes, then you know you have a strong enough friendships that it can survive temporary inconsistent reciprocity. However, if your answer is no, then what is it that keeps you in this friendship? What is your motivation to continue this relationship?

Once you've assessed, you've explored, and you've identified that one of your relationships is not reciprocal, so now what? It is up to you to decide if you want to cut ties completely, confront your friend about the unbalance and how you feel about it, or you can decrease the amount of energy and effort you put into this relationship and simply prioritize this friendship less. There is still something in this relationship you feel is rewarding to you, and you don't want to let go completely, but you are willing to let go slightly. That's okay. Not every relationship will have the same level of closeness, connection, and time and energy spent. We have many relationships that fill different needs at different times.

Your time is valuable, and so is what you bring to your relationships. It's okay to be selective in how and who you spend your time with. Who is worth your time? Who is worth investing in? As we get older, there is personal time, and less time to spend with friends. So, when that opportunity is there to be social and catch up on your relationships, it's important that the relationships deserve it. Not every relationship will be worth it, and not every relationship is meant to last forever. Certain relationships are meant to fill a specific purpose and time in your life.

We all need people in our life who contribute to our growth in some way. Whether it's simply by being support in a time of need, or someone who challenges us to expand our way of thinking, regardless of what it is, it's important and healthy to have people around you that help you thrive and grow. When we allow people in who do not add to our life in anyway, or simply take without giving back, we are susceptible to stagnation, burnout, or even a poor sense of self. To really take inventory of the quality of your friendships with the goal of eliminating any non-reciprocal or toxic friends, it means we value ourselves enough to believe we deserve better, we deserve to be treated the way we treat others.

This dance of ongoing, reciprocal giving and receiving is a characteristic of all extraordinarily successful relationships. When it is fully integrated into a relationship, the motivation that drives each partner is that of "enlightened self-interest." This term refers to the deep understanding and trust that when I give freely and unconditionally to another, my own well-being is enhanced, regardless of how they respond. It's the trust that the return to me comes through my act of giving, not as a result of it. And when two people are simultaneously operating from this understanding, there's no telling what they can create together.

A relationship cannot survive on its own. It needs the care and nurturing of two adults, giving to each other in a way that creates a mutually beneficial connection. To foster a deep and loving relationship, there needs to be:

1. Kind, constant, and honest communication. Without talking, your relationship will not survive. The more you communicate, the closer you will be.

2. The willingness to work through difficulties and disagreements. Giving up, even if you don't walk out the door, is not the path to happiness. You must face the discomfort that comes with differing opinions and ideas.

3. A sense of humor, some fun, and a bit of distraction from the rigors of daily life. You can't spend all your free time "working" on your

relationship—don't make it a hobby. Discuss what you like to do, where you'd like to go, and how you both like to have fun. Then do it.

4. Sharing life lessons with the one you love. When you discover something about life, or you make a self-correcting move that is healthy for your relationship, let your partner know. You'll be surprised by the positive response.

5. Emotional support, validation, and compliments. If you don't feel that your partner likes and respects you, there will not be a strong connection. You have to lift each other up and let each other know the depth of your caring.

6. Love, intimacy, and romance. These are the cornerstones of a loving

relationship. Being great roommates just won't cut it. There has to be the desire to be together as a couple. You may think the spark has gone, but there are too many ways to rekindle it. All you have to do is try.

7. Sharing goals and dreams that resonate with both of you. We are happier when we are working toward a goal than when we have achieved one. Make sure you always have something to look forward to and that you are pursuing it as a couple.

8. Compassion and forgiveness. These will show you the way through a difficult time. If you are together for a while, there will be losses, challenges, and some things that you just can't fix. Weathering the storms together is a big part of what relationships are all about.

9. A mutual desire to step outside the box. The tried-and-true is good, but the never- attempted-before may be better. Couples who share new experiences together develop a stronger bond.

10. Being able to admit mistakes and to talk about them. We all screw up. Learning to understand and let go of mistakes that you or your partner make will turn your life around and give you more time for joy.

Just as we need to breathe to survive, your love needs reciprocation to flourish.

# Chapter Six

The first time we see an example of a love relationship in the Bible, the one between Adam and Eve, it surprisingly doesn't show a display of passion. Not in the sense you would think.

Many times, when we think of love, we think about the butterflies we feel floating in the oceanic waves of our stomach when meet the person we think is "the one." We think about the goosebumps that travel our spine or race the length of our arms when they come into our presence. We think about the moments when our body is aroused, and we want to be intimately joined to our partner. We think about the soaring good times, the unlimited possibilities of a bright future, and any and all things that project a positive or pleasant emotion. But, if you've been in a relationship for any decent amount of time, then you know that even fairytales have scary moments, and wicked characters. Even the most beautiful rainbows fade. Nothing is perfect all of the time. So many people desire the rainbow but do not want the rain.

So, what keeps a relationship breathing when life threatens to pull the plug on it? How do you find your way back to each other and reset the love once trust has been tattered? Once the relationship's security has been breached? Once one person has mentally exited the relationship?

Well, I can tell you that no amount of passion is sufficient enough to rescue a relationship that is on the brink of disaster. What will always bring two people back to the table to keep trying is, purpose and vision. This goes back to the marriage of Adam and Eve. When Adam was created, God gave him a purpose. He announced that purpose, allowed Adam to operate in that purpose, and then put him to sleep to create his purpose partner, Eve. When Eve was brought before Adam, it was Adam who announced what her purpose was in his life. So, the first thing we must consider is, the man must know the purpose of the woman he has chosen in his life. If a man pursues a woman simply based on passion, that relationship is more than likely going to die at some point. But, when he knows his purpose/vision and his woman's purpose/vision, and two people know what their collective purpose/vision is, it will always serve as the relationship's ventilator, thereby, should be the first thing they resort to when the relationship begins to lack the air to survive. This is crucial, because if a person doesn't first love, understand, and accept your purpose, they don't deserve your passion. Typically, people will resort to passion to fix issues that run deeper than twenty or thirty minutes in the bed. When you are with your purpose partner, your vision partner, the relationship has a chance of surviving if you can find your way back to purpose, or your vision, for the love.

What is a purpose partner? One way to know you have met your purpose partner is if they are constantly pushing you to greatness and challenging you to be better even if you think you have already made it. They are divinely sent by God to help you live in your purpose by helping you achieve a level of greatness you can't reach on your own. They are not intimidated by the visions God gives you and are behind the scenes helping you strategize how to bring those visions to pass. They help you carry out God's assignment and are there when it's time to do something in conjunction with your purpose. They jump in where needed and even if they don't get public recognition for the work they do, they remain faithful to their purpose which is to serve your purpose. When you have found such a person, it makes fighting for the relationship worthwhile.

One of my favorite Biblical examples of Purpose Partners is that of David and Jonathan. The Bible reads in I Samuel 18:1-4, *"After David had finished talking with Saul, Jonathan became one in spirit with David, and he loved him as himself. From that day Saul kept David with him and did not let him return home to his family. And Jonathan made a covenant with David because he loved him as himself. Jonathan took off the robe he was wearing and gave it to David, along with his tunic, and even his sword, his bow, and his belt."*

This text reveals why it is so important to fall in love with a person based on purpose. Your purpose partners are not only linked to your heart, but they are also linked to your spirit. The scripture says Jonathan became one in spirit with David. It's great to have someone love and take care of your heart, but that person may not be necessarily linked to your spirit. Your ordained purpose partners are joined to your spirit with spiritual ties that are stronger than fleshly ties, and those ties aren't easily broken. It is tremendously easier to remove someone from your life than it is removing them from your spirit. Thereby, if a purpose partner is linked to your spirit, whatever is conceived in your spirit (purpose related), they are immediately attached to it and will ensure that you give birth to it. Their only question is, "How can I help?"

Your purpose partners will take risks with you even if it puts them at risk. It's best friend behavior and your purpose partner should be your best friend. Using the text above not as an example of a love relationship, but as a picture of what it looks like to have a best friend. Jonathan was so connected to David's purpose that he was willing to risk his own life if necessary. Jonathan went against his own father, King Saul, and told David, whatever he needed him to do, he would do it. *(Read I Samuel 20: 1-42)* Don't miss the dynamics of this. Saul, who was initially fond of David, eventually hated him, and his own son, Jonathan, was willing to lose his life so that David's life and purpose could be spared. Is the person you're with willing to delay, let alone give up, their own dreams, goals, and desires to make sure your purposed is fulfilled? Not only was Jonathan willing to risk his life, but he also produced a plan to save his life. Let that marinate. A purpose partner will help you strategize so you can identify the many options that are available for you to be successful. Imagine if a football team only had one coach and that coach was responsible for designing plays, calling plays, and watching the field to make sure the plays were executed. There would be a lot fewer people gunning to be coaches if that much pressure was on their shoulders. Such as the same for a person with purpose. A lot less people would be willing to live in their purpose, no matter how much they may want to, if they had to do everything alone. Here is a takeaway point: **YOU CAN'T DO LIFE BY YOURSELF.** Your purpose partner gets in the huddle with you and helps you strategize for the win even if they don't get the praise for it. What is a coach without a defensive or offensive coordinator? What is a purpose without purpose partners?

When Jonathan made the decision to be in covenant with David, the scripture says he took off his robe, his tunic, his sword, bow, belt. Wow, what a gesture to make. Most of us have trouble getting people to spend a dollar with our new business, let alone make a sacrifice to give us what we need even if they themselves need it. It is for certain Jonathan could have replaced those garments and weapons, but the notable thing here is that he took it off immediately upon seeing the need and gave it away. When you are in covenant with your purpose partner, you'll notice that they don't wait to think about *if* they are going to give, they give to the cause right away void of hesitation. It is safe to assume Jonathan's robe and tunic were crafted and stitched with the most expensive fabrics and threads. He was the son of the King. Is your significant other willing to give up something they love to assist you with your purpose? Can your woman hold off getting the new Louis Vuitton bag or your man his brand-new pair of Jordan's if it serves your collective purpose? Jonathan had no reluctance in him taking it off and handing it over. He did it with joy and gladness. Why? Because he was in covenant—because he was linked to David's purpose. Purpose partners have an innate desire to see you have all you need to be effective in your purpose. Even if it delays their gratification.

While I could go on further into what a purpose partner does, I want to make another point that serves as a bullet point to the main point. Here it is: The enemy's most successful entry point into the life of a believer is through another person. When you are thinking about leaving your relationship or allowing outsider people to interfere, be sure to ask yourself if you are opening the door for the enemy to come in and unravel the seams of your purpose. Friends, you have to be tenacious in guarding your relationship with your purpose partner, because in doing so, you are guarding your purpose. While Jesus preached to the multitudes, he had seventy disciples, twelve of the seventy were considered His chosen, and only three were truly a part of his inner circle. In the case of a love relationship, the only people in the circle should be you and your significant other. No other people. That person is the chosen ONE. You can't successfully fulfill your God ordained purpose with more than one person in that role. It just doesn't work that way and the sooner you realize that the sooner you'll be on your way to living an amazing life with the one you love.

Whatever area your relationship is struggling in, do yourself a favor, grab the hand of your partner and get to the table of purpose quickly. The longer you focus on the minors of your relationship, the enemy will keep you blinded to the major damage it's doing. What damage is it doing? It's delaying purpose. It's potentially canceling it, too. It is time to say goodbye to anything that's causing the confusion in your relationship or that is negatively contributing to what God has His hand on. With all of this being said, no book, Pastor, preacher, teacher, or life coach can convince you to do this until you get to a point where the problems of the relationship are no longer worth sacrificing another moment of your destiny together.

Purpose sets the guidelines so that no party is confused or misguided. Purpose sets the expectations. Purpose leaves no stones unturned, and it leaves no questions not answered. When you meet your purpose partner, it's important for you to affirm that as often as you can, because again, it's the purpose the enemy will be after.

Here's the reality: in five years, you will not be the same. Better or worse, you'll be different. Success in a relationship happens on purpose and never by accident. **So, to** reach a certain point in your marriage, you'll have to work at it. In marriage, success only happens if you're both committed to the same purpose—the same vision. Amos 3:3 asks, "Do two walk together unless they have agreed to do so?" If you're not in agreement, your marriage, the longest journey of your life, will be a constant challenge. Keeping those facts in mind, I want you to know that finding the purpose for your marriage means starting with the big questions. Not "Where will we live?" or "How many kids should we have?" but "Why are we here?"

The answer is simple. God created us for relationship, to have a relationship with Him and a relationship with each other. This is reflected in Jesus' teaching about the two greatest commandments: to love God and to love people. Relationships are why we exist, and He wants us to have successful relationships. On the other hand, the enemy wants to destroy relationships by either separating us from God or separating us from each other—especially from our spouse. Satan is always trying to divide, and he does that by separation.

We see this in Genesis with Adam and Eve. God put them in a perfect paradise, but Satan convinces them that God meant evil towards them. He falsely accuses God. He tries to divide Adam and Eve from God, and he goes further by speaking first to Eve, in order to divide Adam and Eve from each other. He does this to couples today in so many different ways. Some of you reading this book may have already found yourself divided from your spouse. Somewhere along the way the enemy may have gotten to you and convinced you that you'd be better off by yourself. With purpose in mind, we know that's a lie.

The second thing the devil does is substitution. He shows the fruit to Adam and

Eve and tells them they didn't need God; they only need the fruit. Today, He makes us believe things will make us happier: money, a new job, a new spouse. He is always trying to get us to substitute things for our marriage or for God. Here's the cold part: the substitution always looks and sounds better. Sure, you can abandon your marriage and your purpose partner, take a risk, and go with the substitution; but is that a risk you're willing to take? For some of you, it has taken you a while to find your purpose partner. Are you going to allow a tough time to divide you?

Separation and substitution are the Devil's viruses for marriage. But God's plan for marriage is relationship—to bring us closer to our spouse, and to bring us closer to Him. His plan for our life is that we love Him and love people, especially our family. Satan's plan is to make us lonely and divided and always unsatisfied. We end up chasing after things. God's plan is for us to pursue Him and pursue relationship. The opportunity to love God and each other is the reason God put you together. It doesn't get any more complicated than that.

| Homework |

1) What is our relationship's vision?

_____

_____

_____

_____

_____

_____

_____

_____

_____

_____

_____

_____

2) What ways can you avoid being
separated from your vision?

_____

_____

_____

_____

_____

_____

_____

_____

_____

_____

_____

_____

3) What ways can you protect your relationship's vision?

_____

_____

_____

_____

_____

_____

_____

_____

_____

_____

_____

_____

_____

4) Is our relationship's purpose worth
fighting for? Why or why not?

_____

_____

_____

_____

_____

_____

_____

_____

_____

_____

_____

_____

5) If we call it quits, who and what will be affected? It is worth it? Why or why not?

_____

_____

_____

_____

_____

_____

_____

_____

_____

_____

_____

_____

# Chapter Seven

What is reality but a concept unique to each of us? Can anything be classified as real when our perceptions differ on so many things? Just because we see something a particular way does not make it so. We can be so insistent sometimes that our way of seeing something is better than someone else's way.

Keep an open mind at all times and remember that a point of view is always valuable to each individual. I always used to class myself as someone who was 'realistic' but after contemplating this further I realized that the term 'realistic' means something quite different entirely.

Let's take the example of war. There are some people who believe that war is necessary sometimes to get peace and then in order to keep the peace. There are other people who will believe that war is evil and should never be entered into no matter what. Who is right? Is war right or wrong? That's just an example and I'm not here to answer that question—especially with what's happening with Russia and Ukraine right now.

There is no such thing as reality. There is only 'your' version of it which is your perception. Remember, what you believe to be true is only as true as your worldly experience and it doesn't go any further than that. Even many scientific theories are just that; they are theories. It doesn't make them absolute fact.

Everyday scientists are making discoveries that are forcing them to throw out the old textbooks and write new ones. As much as we think we may know how life works, I promise the limited knowledge will continue to be re-written over the coming centuries.

It's important to note that how you choose to perceive things is how they come across to you.

I remember hearing a story about a woman who shared that a few days after her son's suicide she had to go to the store to pick something up. She was broken and sad and could barely force herself to go. As she arrived at the store she saw everyone around her happy and hustling to get things done and she said she wanted to scream out "STOP! Don't you know what has happened? Don't you know that my son is dead? Don't you see that my world has come crashing down around me?"

Now, let me tell you the view of someone else who happened to be at the store that day, but who had no idea what had just happened to this woman. The other person came into the store and was in a hurry to grab something. They were rushing through the store and got in line with the woman who was preoccupied with the thoughts of her loss and not paying attention. They were frustrated with that woman thinking, "What is your problem? I am in a hurry here and you are holding me up? Seriously, why do you have to inconvenience everyone else because you can't get it together?"

That story paints perfectly the picture of what happens every day around us, and I see it happen all the time with people. Someone views events around them and they immediately try to interpret those events using just the data they have at that point mixed with the emotions they are dealing with that day. Then they form an opinion of a person, or a situation, and they believe it to be true. As simple as that, they have formed the way they see the world around them. How sad would it be for everyone to suddenly have the entire story, all the facts, all the reasons, all the details – only to find out that everything they thought to be true wasn't the case at all?

The reality is, no one can ever have all of the facts in every situation because usually there just isn't time to gather them all. What they can do is modify the way that they choose to view things. Rather than taking half information and painting the picture to be one that is negative, hurtful, or sad, what if instead they chose to look for the positive meaning that might exist? What if they chose to look for the way to view it in a light that was happy, and optimistic, and hopeful? Which of those two options is likely to help them feel the happiest?

Consider these random scenarios and my suggestions in dealing with them:

When someone is rude to those around them, instead of focusing on the fact that they are a jerk, we should recognize that they are insecure and need validation to feel good about themselves.

When someone is having a private conversation with someone else, instead of thinking they are talking negatively about you, we should choose to be happy that they are able to get the support from each other for whatever is going on in their life.

When a manager forgets to tell you, they noticed your hard work, instead of thinking they don't appreciate all you do, you may consider the fact that they might be overwhelmed themselves. Even though they didn't voice it, that doesn't mean they don't feel it, because their delegating to you is a clear sign that they need you and trust you.

When someone walks past you without saying hello, instead of thinking they don't like you, consider that they could just be running behind. Send good wishes their way to help them make it on time.

Can you see the difference you can make by simply changing the way you perceive things? Happiness, my friends, is an *inside* job. Don't allow yourself to interpret things negatively when the reality is that it may have nothing to do with you at all – 99.9 percent of the time they don't. If everyone knew each other's back stories of their lives and their struggles, then they would recognize that everyone is grateful to have each other as their friend and everyone is grateful for their support.

If we want to find happiness in our lives we have to give each other the benefit of the doubt. We have to give people the benefit of the doubt. We have to try and see the world through a positive interpretation of what is going wrong that day. We have to try and see that scenario where people are good, with good hearts, and good intentions. Life is so much better when you do, and the world around you is a far more beautiful place to live. Your view of this world is up to you.

# Chapter Eight

The quality of our lives is determined by the choices we make which career path we take, which partner we choose, the lifestyle we embrace. Just as you have the responsibility and the power to make choices about your wardrobe, your relationships, or the car you drive, you have the same responsibility and power to choose your attitude and approach to life.

One theory in psychology research suggests that we all have a happiness "set-point" that determines our overall well-being. We oscillate around this set point, becoming happier when something positive happens or the opposite, afterwards returning to equilibrium. But this set-point, to a certain extent, can be *reset*. Although our general mood levels and well-being are partially determined by factors like genetics and upbringing, 40 percent of our happiness is within our control, according to some experts, and a large body of research in the field of positive psychology has shown that happiness is a choice that anyone can make. As psychologist William James put it, "The greatest discovery of any generation is that a human can alter his life by altering his attitude."

With that said, a great day starts with you.

This mantra is what I speak since I've started this enjoyable journey. Early on, I noticed how quickly I gravitate more often towards positive things. Shows like "Undercover Boss" captured my attention and held my interest. I'm a huge fan of positive stories told by humble, like- minded people. I worship God, the one who created the sun, moon, and stars, which radiate and represents all positive things. The sun burns inside my soul. The stars allow only a glimpse into the mysteries of the unknown, and the moonlight shows nothing is so far away that is unattainable. By no means am I perfect, mistakes are forever a part of my DNA. Right and wrong and pessimistic vs. optimistic are daily struggles just like good against evil.

Taking accountability for your actions will help you to understand the actual meaning of *a great day starts with you, within you.*

To that same point: happiness starts with you...within you.

# Chapter Nine

Most people have never learned how to communicate. Without this skill, a person is handicapped in an intimate relationship. Without being able to express themselves and listen to another, partners cannot achieve intimacy. By developing your communication skills, you and your partner will be able to establish and preserve a loving, respectful relationship between two people who love each other.

One of the biggest problems in communicating is that most couples have a basic misconception of what the purpose of communication is. Most approach talking with a partner as a debate in which each presents a preconceived version of the reality of what is going on between the two partners.

The fault with this approach is the mistaken assumption that either partner can go into the conversation with an accurate perception of reality. This is not possible because neither person has the necessary information to determine what reality is, that is: what is going on between them.

Everyone knows that communication is simply a matter of talking and listening. However, most of us mistakenly believe that the matter of communicating is simple. We fail to realize that rather than involving innate abilities, communication involves specific skills can be learned and developed in ourselves in order to talk with and listen to our loved ones.

Rule #1 to follow when going into a conversation with your partner: Disarm. In other words, give up the need to be right! You are not going into a battle that you have to win.

This is not to say that you will have to compromise or surrender. This is not to say that you can't be angry, frustrated, or provoked. You have a right to all of your thoughts and feelings.

Just consider that your partner may have something to say that is worth listening to and considering. This conversation is not a battleground where you must prove that you are right; it is not a fight that you must win.

Going into a conversation, there is only one reality that a person can be sure of: you can know what your own thoughts, feelings and perceptions are. You can be sure of nothing else: not the other person's thoughts, feelings, or perceptions; not even the reality of what is going on between the two of you.

The only thing that you and your partner each needs to bring to the conversation is something that each of you can be sure of your own thoughts, feelings, and perceptions. However, talking personally about yourself is often more challenging than you might think.

It is an unfortunate reality that, within all couples, one person is victimized by the other. As a result, the focus of many of their discussions is on blaming each other. In your effort to talk about yourself, avoid the temptation to lapse into attacking, accusing, criticizing, or blaming your partner.

It is also important to recognize your irrational feelings. Don't dismiss them as being inappropriate, immature, or meaningless. Try to talk about the feelings that you would much rather skip over. The feelings that you fear will cause you embarrassment or humiliation should you disclose them. For example, if you feel hurt or disappointed discuss these feelings with your partner. Avoid the temptation to defend yourself by becoming victimized and righteous. This is not about how you shouldn't hurt or be disappointed. It is about the simple truth that you're hurt or disappointed, and that it is causing you emotional pain.

People often feel embarrassed to talk about what they want. Not the easy wants: I want to go to that new restaurant, I want a new jacket, I want to go on a trip. But the personal wants that come from deep down in you where you feel the most vulnerable: I want you to complement me, I want to be affectionate with you, I want to have a baby with you. Many of us have grown up feeling ashamed of our wants. However, the more that you communicate on this level, the more in touch with yourself you will be–the more authentic you will be as a person–the closer your partner will be able to feel to you. When you and your partner communicate on this personal level, many of the trivial issues between you vanish. It becomes apparent that they were merely inconsequential issues meant to distract you in your relationship.

Finally, talk to your partner with the decency and respect with which you talk to anyone else. Most people have a special way of communicating that they reserve for their partners. What makes it special is that it includes abusive behaviors such as: being complaining, demanding, bossy, irritable, sarcastic, childish, parental, condescending...to name a few. When you are talking with your partner, stop and ask yourself: "Would I be talking like this to anyone else?" Do you hear yourself complaining (I'm so tired!) or demanding (Get me a drink of water!!) or deferring (What should I order for dinner?) in ways you never hear yourself with other people? Try to treat your partner with the respect and decency with which you treat any other person.

Listening is a skill that needs to be learned and developed. Just because we hear does not mean that we are listening. Only when we listen with an unconditional interest in understanding the person who is talking to us, can we truly get to know that person. Listening is entirely about the person you are listening to. Put aside your point of view. Your thoughts, opinions, or reactions to what the other person is saying are both irrelevant and inappropriate. The person talking is not looking to you for advice or guidance. What they truly need is to be heard so that they feel that they are being seen. When you put yourself aside, that is when you focus on what your partner is saying rather than on how you are reacting, you are making yourself available to listen to your partner. As your partner talks, try to sense what it feels like to be him or her.

Try to feel what your partner is experiencing. Empathize. Listen with your heart. When he or she relates an incident to you, try to feel how he or she felt in the situation. Make a special effort to empathize with what your partner is currently feeling while talking with you.

As you listen to your partner with empathy and feel what he or she feels, you gain compassion for him or her as a person. You feel for him or her as a human being with personal pain and struggles like the rest of us. You gain a new perspective. When you feel for your partner's issues, your own personal over-reactions to them seem unimportant. Giving advice or being judgmental suddenly seems condescending and patronizing. Acting hurt or victimized suddenly seems childish and self-indulgent. From this perspective, you see your partner as a separate person who you care about deeply as he or she deals with his-her own issues in life.

In the process of talking personally about yourself as your partner truly listened, it is likely that you both came to a deeper understanding of what you were experiencing and feeling. Likewise, as your partner talked personally to you with you truly listening, both of you came to a deeper understanding of your partner's experiences and feelings. This level of insight and understanding along with the feelings of empathy and compassion that accompany it, help clarify much of the confusion that exists within the couple.

The deeper awareness of each other eliminates many of the misconceptions, misinterpretations and miscommunications that go into creating this confusion. What remains is a clearer picture of yourselves and of the reality of your relationship.

There are several negative forms of communication to be aware of. Make sure that you are not engaging in any of these because they contaminate the communication process. Communication should bring you and your partner closer to each other. It should be used to break down the barriers that keep you apart, not to build up fortifications between you. I have concluded that if in my next relationship my partner can't talk to me right, I don't want to be talked to at all. I don't have the patience to accept certain forms of communication because it compromises my happiness.

One of the most effective techniques that couples use to manipulate, control, and punish each other is intimidation. According to the dictionary, to intimidate is to frighten into submission. Interestingly enough, couples report that the behaviors they are intimidated by are not those that are overt and aggressive. Partners are frightened by the subtle covert behaviors that leave them feeling guilty and responsible for their mate's unhappiness. During a conversation between a couple, if one partner responds by being miserable, self-hating or self-destructive, it is virtually impossible for the other partner not to submit. The conversation is over; the intimidating partner has won. But in reality, both people have suffered defeats. The dictionary goes on to say that to intimidate "implies reduction to a state where the spirit is broken, or all courage is lost."

Watch out for ways that you might be communicating from a childish or parental stance. Childish communications involve deferring and submitting, looking for direction or definition, being servile or subservient, seeking approval and/or criticism. Parental communications involve directing and dominating, being condescending and assertive, acting judgmental and critical. None of this has a place in the communications between two independent adults in an equal relationship. Be respectful of yourself and respectful of your partner in the way that you speak to each other.

Pay attention to what your actions are saying. Make your actions and words match. In other words, be truthful in how you communicate both verbally and non-verbally if you want to foster happiness in the environment of your relationship.

# Chapter Ten

It's in our nature to care about what other people think. We live in a state of perpetual fear over the thoughts and opinions of others. It's sad, but our daily actions are often motivated by obtaining the approval of others. There's an obsession with making sure we don't disappoint those around us, and this is most usually in exchange for our own happiness.

Think about all that you do for everyone else, and then think about what you do for yourself. How much time do you spend caring about other people's needs before you pay mind to your own? This is a common occurrence found among females in motherhood, sure, as tending to children is in the maternal nature of women. However, this trend has been present more recently in younger generations and our youths compromising their goals, dreams, and aspirations to succumb to the desires of those around them, or to fit the mold of what's practical.

College students are settling for majors they don't love, just to satisfy the wishes of their parents; while graduates are accepting job offers in positions they hate, just so their parents will cease the pressure and will have something "good" to tell their friends at dinner parties. Despite having so much life to live, the younger generation has fallen victim to the epidemic of settling, of putting their desires and wants to the wayside, in order to fulfill those of their parents, friends and peers.

Of course, helping others is admirable. It's a beautiful thing to see humans caring for one another and putting the needs of others before their own. It's a testament to brotherhood and to humanity. But what happens when your selflessness becomes an innate characteristic of yourself? What happens when you become so compelled to please everyone else that you dismiss your own happiness? What happens when you witness your life becoming a composite of the favors and demands of others?

There will come a point in your life (and hopefully, that point is right now) when it's imperative that you learn how to stick up for yourself and learn that to be selfish for the well-being of the self is, in fact, acceptable. As you become more of an adult with more to lose and less time to spend on this Earth, you must become stronger and more confident in expressing how you feel. You must learn to stick up for yourself to make sure that you are not being taken advantage of. However, I know as well as anyone that it's difficult to dictate to others on matters they don't wish to hear. The pain of letting someone down, disappointing them, just doesn't seem worth the freedom that comes with saying, "No."

Whether it's a stranger on the plane or your little sister, telling someone something he or she doesn't want to hear can be extremely hard. We are empathetic and compassionate beings, who understand what it feels like to be let down, or even rejected, and we don't like to bring sorrow onto others any more than we do onto ourselves.

Of course, being selfish is not virtuous. I'm not condoning that you completely disregard the needs of others and only take care of yourself. It's utter selfishness that leads to the loss of friends and betrayal of family, but you must find a middle ground. You must decipher when it's okay to be selfish, when it's okay to take care of yourself first.

The first step in doing so is understanding the motives of individuals and what they are asking of you. You are too young to be making sacrifices and compromises, before your future has even had a chance to play out. Don't let others take advantage of your selfless nature and kind heart. While your friends and family may not be consciously taking advantage of your warm and giving traits, it's human nature to worry about yourself before others, and they may not very well realize what they are doing.

You must learn to recognize when people need your help and when they simply want it. Here are a few factors to consider when determining whether the actions of another are a result of need or want:

- Your friend isn't going to remove you from his or her life because you couldn't pick her up at the airport. If you aren't busy and you can spare the time and the gas to pick up a friend, do it. But if you are busy and heading to the station is going to inconvenience you, your friend is not going to hold it against you forever. People won't remember the trivial times you couldn't lend a helping hand as much as they remember all the times you did.

- People move on. While your parents may be disappointed for a few weeks after you tell them you aren't studying their major of choice, they will get over it. Time heals all, and eventually, people will move past your choice to go another direction and continue focusing on their own lives, apart from their wants and desires for you.

- You must remember that you are the hero, or female protagonist, of your life, not the supporting character. This is your life and your needs come before anyone else's. While it's great to help others and make people feel good, it's important that you are not giving away everything you have without getting anything in return.

You are the only one who knows what you need and what is going to make you happy. Why would listening to others and following their wishes and demands benefit you? As your aspirations and desires become more unique, it will become more important for you to stick up for yourself to protect those dreams.

So often I hear of people unsuccessfully trying to make someone else happy. They give and give and give, but nothing seems to work.

They actually *believe* that the more they sacrifice, the more it shows they care, even though it couldn't be further from the truth. You can give all you want, but you can't give something that you don't already have. If you haven't achieved happiness for yourself, then how could you help someone else achieve their happiness? It's impossible. You may be able to provide some short-term pleasure, but you can't teach someone something that you have no understanding of.

When it comes to first achieving happiness for yourself, I'm reminded of the lecture they often give on airplanes about oxygen masks. They always tell you that in times of emergency you should put your oxygen mask on first, *then* help your neighbors put on their masks. The reasoning is simple: if you don't put on your oxygen mask first, you suffer a greater likelihood of dying; and you can't help anyone once you're dead.

In the same way, you can't make someone happy if you're depressed. You have to take care of yourself first before taking care of others. Anything else is a recipe for disaster for the both of you.

Some people try to do good and charitable things with the *expectation* that it will automatically make them and the other person happier. Of course, I don't want to discourage you from helping others, but I want you to know that there is a point where it may be best to cut your losses and walk away. Some people can be emotional leeches, they depend on your pity in order to manipulate you. It's sad, but some people don't want to be happy simply because they don't want to act or take responsibility for their own lives. They want someone else to do all the work for them, but that too is impossible. You can only influence and encourage people to find happiness, you can't force it onto them.

# Chapter Eleven

If you are going to live a happy life, you are going to have to discover the things that promote and trigger happiness. CNN wrote an article that suggest ways to do that. First, you start by changing your attitude.

A Harvard University study found that optimists are not only happier but are 50% less likely to have heart disease, a heart attack, or a stroke. It turns out that keeping a positive outlook offers protection against cardiovascular disease. The science doesn't fare as well for pessimists. They have lower levels of happiness compared with optimists and are three times as likely to develop health problems as they age, researchers say.

The article goes on to advise one to learn from people who are already happy. A study was done, and research showed that Denmark has earned the top spot on the European Commission's "Eurobarometer" for well-being and happiness every year since 1973. And when the United Nations went on the hunt for the happiest nation in the world, it ranked Denmark No. 1.

So, what makes Danes more satisfied with their lives? Sure, things like life expectancy, gross domestic product, and a low-corruption rate help. But the overall level of happiness in Denmark has more to do with the generosity that's common among citizens, their freedom to make life choices and a strong social support system,

The Danes strike a great work-life balance, which ups their happiness level. Simply put: They don't overwork. In fact, the average workweek in Denmark is 33 hours --

only 2% of Danes work more than 40 hours a week.

Almost 80% of mothers in Denmark return to work after having a child, but they balance their free time between families, weekly happy hour with their girlfriends and participating in community club programs.

- **Focus on experiences.**

Danes also pay less attention to gadgets and things and more attention to building memories. Studies show that people who focus on experiences over "things" have higher levels of satisfaction, long after the moment of the experience has passed. Too much stuff tends often leads to debt, not to mention the time and stress associated with keeping up all those gadgets, cars, properties, clothes, etc. Researchers say when people focus on experiences, they feel a greater sense of vitality or "being alive" during the experience and afterward. It also brings you mentally closer to the people around you, which may contribute to your happiness boost.

- **Just start laughing.**

Research shows that laughing doesn't just signal happiness, it produces it. When we laugh, our stress hormones decrease, and our endorphins rise. Endorphins are the same brain chemicals associated with the "runner's high" you get from exercise. Laughing is also good for your heart. A study found that only 8% of heart patients who were made to laugh daily had a second heart attack within a year, compared with 42% of the non-laughers. Studies show our bodies can't differentiate between fake and real laughter; you'll get the health boost either way. So, you can even fake it until you make it. Laugh in your car, in the shower -- force yourself to start laughing a few minutes every day.

Consider this list of <u>Intentional Actions to Choose Happiness Today</u>. Embrace one new action item... practice all of them... or simply use them as inspiration to discover your own.

1. **Count your blessings.**

   Happy people choose to focus on the positive aspects of life rather than the negative. They set their minds on specific reasons to be grateful. They express it when possible. And they quickly discover there is always, always, something to be grateful for.

2. **Carry a smile.**

   A smile is a wonderful beautifier. But more than that, studies indicate that making an emotion-filled face carries influence over the feelings processed by the brain. Our facial expression can influence our brain in just the same way our brains influence our face. In other words, you can actually program yourself to experience happiness by choosing to smile. Not to mention, all the pretty smiles you'll receive in return for flashing yours is also guaranteed to increase your happiness level.

3. **Speak daily affirmation into your life.**

   Affirmations are positive thoughts accompanied with affirmative beliefs and personal statements of truth. They are recited in the first person, present tense *("I am...")*. Affirmations used daily can release stress, build confidence, and improve outlook. For maximum effectiveness, affirmations should be chosen carefully, be based in truth, and address current needs.

4. **Wake up on your terms.**

   Most of us have alarm clocks programmed because of the expectations of others: a workplace, a school, or a waking child. That's not going to change. But that doesn't mean we have to lose control over our mornings in the process. Wake up just a little bit early and establish an empowering, meaningful, morning routine. Start each day on your terms. The next 23 hours will thank you for it.

5. **Hold back a complaint.**
The next time you want to lash out in verbal complaint towards a person, a situation, or yourself, don't. Instead, humbly keep it to yourself. You'll diffuse an unhealthy, unhappy environment. But more than that, you'll experience joy by choosing peace in a difficult situation.

**6. Practice one life-improving discipline.**

There is happiness and fulfillment to be found in personal growth. To know that you have intentionally devoted time and energy to personal improvement is one of the most satisfying feelings you'll ever experience. Embrace and practice at least one act of self-discipline each day. This could be exercise, budgeting, or guided learning... whatever your life needs today to continue growing. Find it. Practice it. Celebrate it.

**7. Use your strengths.**

Each of us have natural talents, strengths, and abilities. And when we use them effectively, we feel alive and comfortable in our skin. They help us find joy in our being and happiness in our design. So, embrace your strengths and choose to operate within your giftedness each day. If you need to find this outlet outside your employment, by all means, find this outlet.

8. **Accomplish one important task.** Because happy people choose happiness, they take control over their lives. They don't make decisions based on a need to pursue joy. Instead, they operate out of the satisfaction they have already chosen. They realize there are demands on their time, helpful pursuits to accomplish, and important contributions to make to the world around them. Choose one important task that you can accomplish each day. And find joy in your contribution.

9. **Eat a healthy meal/snack.** We are spiritual, emotional, and mental beings. We are also physical bodies. Our lives cannot be separated into its parts. As a result, one aspect

always influences the others. For example, our physical bodies will always have impact over our spiritual and emotional well-being. Therefore, caring for our physical well-being can have significant benefit for our emotional standing. One simple action to choose happiness today is to eat healthy foods. Your physical body will thank you... and so will your emotional well-being.

## 10. Treat others well.

Everyone wants to be treated kindly. But more than that, deep down, we also want to treat others with the same respect that we would like given to us. Treat everyone you meet with kindness, patience, and grace. The Golden Rule is a powerful standard. It benefits the receiver. But also brings growing satisfaction in yourself as you seek to treat others as you would like to be treated.

**11. Meditate.**

Find time alone in solitude. As our world increases in speed and noise, the ability to withdraw becomes even more essential. Studies confirm the importance and life-giving benefits of meditation. So, take time to make time. And use meditation to search inward, connect spiritually, and improve your happiness today.

**12. Search for benefit in your pain.** This life can be difficult. Nobody escapes without pain. At some point— in some way—we all encounter it. When you do, remind yourself again that the trials may be difficult, but they will pass. And search deep to find meaning in the pain. Choose to look for the benefits that can be found in your trial. At the very least, perseverance is being built. And an ability to comfort others in their pain is also being developed.

Choose joy and be happy.

Do what you love. Period.

# Chapter Twelve

To be able to remain happy it is essential to have influences in your life that support you and lift you up instead of dragging you down. This is especially true in relationships.

*"The amount of happiness that you have depends on the amount of freedom you have in your heart." ~Thich Nhat Hanh*

If you've been holding onto an old relationship, now is the perfect time to let go. Here's how you can start moving on. Here are nine ways to work towards achieving that:

**1. Practice releasing regrets.**

When a relationship ends, it's tempting to dwell on what you did wrong or what you could have done differently. This might seem productive—like you can somehow change things by rehashing it. You can't. All dwelling does is cause you to suffer. When you start revisiting the past in your head, pull yourself into the moment. Focus on the good things in your current situation: the friends who are there for you and the lessons you've learned that will help you with future relationships. It might help to tell your friends to only let you vent for ten minutes at a time. That way you're free to express your feelings, but not drown in them.

## 2. Work on forgiving yourself.

You might think you made the biggest mistake of your life and if only you didn't do it, you wouldn't be in pain right now. Don't go down that road—there's nothing good down there! Instead, keep reminding yourself that you are human. You're entitled to make mistakes; everyone does. And you will learn from them and use those lessons to improve your life. Also, keep in mind: if you want to feel love again in the future, the first step is to prepare yourself to give and receive it. You can only do that if you feel love toward yourself. And that means forgiving yourself.

**3. Don't think about any time as lost.**

If I looked at my failed marriages as time lost, I'd underestimate all the amazing things I did in that time. If you've been clinging to the past for a while and now feel you've missed out, shift the focus to everything you've gained. You've built great friendships or made great progress in your career. When you focus on the positive, it's easier to move on because you'll feel empowered and not victimized (by your ex, by yourself, or by time.) Whatever happened in the past, it prepared you for now—and now is full of opportunities for growth, peace, and happiness.

**4. Remember the bad as well as the good.**

Brain scientists suggest 20 percent of us suffer from "complicated grief," a persistent sense of longing for someone we lost with romanticized memories of the relationship. Scientists also suggest this is a biological occurrence—that the longing can have an addictive quality to it, actually rooted in our brain chemistry. As a result, we tend to remember everything with reverie, as if it was all sunshine and roses. If your ex broke up with you, it may be even more tempting to imagine she or he was perfect, and you weren't. In all reality, you both have strengths and weaknesses and you both made mistakes. Remember them now.

## 5. Reconnect with who you are outside a relationship.

It's quite possible you lived a fulfilling single life before you got into this relationship. And you felt strong, satisfied, and happy, if not with everything in your life, on the whole. Remember that person now. Reconnect with any people or interests that may have received less attention while you were attached. Your former self attracted your ex, and they're still there inside you. That person will get you through this loss and will attract someone equally amazing in the future, when the time is right. If you can't remember who you were, get to know yourself now. What's important to you? What do you enjoy? What makes you feel alive? If you *never* felt satisfied and happy on your own, use this as opportunity to become the kind of person you'd want to be with, because you're going to be with yourself forever, regardless of your relationship status. And though someone else can complement your life, you are the only one who can fill yourself from the inside out.

## 6. Create separation.

Hope can be a terrible thing if it keeps you stuck in the past. It's not easy to end all contact when you feel attached to someone. Breaking off the friendship might feel like you're ruining your chances at knowing love again. It's helped me to change my hopes to broader terms. So, instead of wanting a specific person to re-enter your life, instead, want love and happiness...whatever that may look like. You *will* know love again. You won't spend the rest of your life alone. In one way or another, you will meet all kinds of people and create all kinds of possibilities for relationships—if you forgive yourself, let go, and open yourself up, that is.

**7. Let yourself feel.**

Losing a relationship can feel like a mini-death, complete with a grieving process.

First, you're shocked and in denial. You don't believe it's over and you hold out hope. Next, you feel hurt and guilty. You should have done things differently. If you did you wouldn't be in this pain. Then, you feel angry and even start bargaining. It would be different if you gave it a second go. You wouldn't be so insecure, defensive, or demanding. Then you might feel depressed and lonely as it hits you how much you've lost. Eventually, you start accepting what happened and shift your focus from the past to the future. You have to go through the feelings as they come, but you can help yourself get through them faster. For example, if you're dwelling in guilt, make forgiving yourself a daily practice. Read books on it, meditate about it, or do what I've done and author a book about your experience.

## 8. Remember the benefits of moving on.

*When you let go, you give yourself peace.*

Everything about holding on is torturous. You regret, you feel ashamed and guilty, you rehash, you obsess—it's all an exercise in suffering. The only way to feel peace is to quiet the thoughts that threaten it. *Letting go opens you up to new possibilities.* When you're holding onto something, you're less open to giving and receiving anything else. If you had your arms wrapped around a huge bucket of water, you wouldn't be able to grab anything other than that bucket or grab anything else that came your way. You might even struggle breathing because you're clutching something all-encompassing with so much effort. You have to give to receive. Give love to get love, share joy to feel joy. It's only possible if you're open and receptive.

## 9. Recognize and replace fearful thoughts.

When you're holding on to a relationship, it's usually more about attachment than love. Love wants for the other person's happiness. Fear wants to hold onto whatever appears to make you happy, so you don't have to feel the alternative. You might not recognize these types of fearful thoughts because they become habitual. Some examples include *I'll never feel loved again. I'll always feel lonely. I am completely powerless.* Replace those thoughts with: *All pain passes eventually. It will be easier if I help them pass by being mindful. I can't always control what happens to me, but I can control how I respond to it.* Your response is your responsibility—negative or positive. Practicing these things will help you to let go, forgive, and move on. The longer you babysit what happened, you will never meet what can happen. I know it can be scary at first to try another relationship after one has failed, but one of life's greatest joys is taking risks. Loving is a risk, but it's a risk worth taking.

# Conclusion

So, having read all you've read, the point I hope you take away is, you deserve to live a life of peace, love, joy, and happiness. I hope something I've written has given you a different outlook and will cause you to make intentional decisions about your life and happiness moving forward.

To recap: Make sure you carefully consider what you let into your mind.

You can for example ask yourself:

- Who are the three most negative people I spend time with?
- What are the three of most negative sources of information I spend time on?

Consider the answers. Then think about how you can start spending less time with one of those people, or information sources, this week. And how you can spend more of the time with one of the most positive sources or people in your life.

**Go slowly.** I have found that when I go too fast, when I try to think, talk, eat and move around in my world really quickly then things don't go too well. Stress builds up. Negative thoughts about anything start to well up and I feel like my own personal power decreases. But if I slow down just for a few minutes – even if I have to force it by walking, talking, and eating slower – then my mind and body calms down, too. It becomes easier to think things through clearly again and easier to find the optimistic and constructive perspective.

**Don't make a mountain out of a molehill.** It's extremely easy to lose perspective, especially if you are stressed and you are going too fast. And so, a molehill can become a big and terrifying mountain in your mind.

A simple three step way to manage situations that threaten to bring you misery is to:

- **Say stop.** In your mind, shout "STOP!" or "NOPE, we are not going down that path again" as soon as thoughts of this kind starts to spin in your head.
- **Breathe.** After you have disrupted the thoughts just be still. Breathe. Relax yourself.
- **Refocus.** Question your mountain building thoughts by talking to someone close to you and getting a more grounded perspective on the

situation by just venting or by getting their input. Or simply ask yourself this to widen your perspective and to chill out: Will this matter in five years? Or even five weeks?

**Don't let vague fears hold you back from doing what you want.** Sometimes you may want to take a chance in life. Start a new habit that feels unfamiliar, your own business on the side, or ask someone out for a date. A common trap when you want to do one of those things is to get lost in vague fears about what could happen if you actually acted. And so, the mind runs wild fueled by fear and it creates nightmare scenarios.

I know. I have been there many times.

So, I have learned to ask myself this: honestly, what is the worst that could happen? When I have figured that out I also spend time on trying to figure out what I could do if that unlikely thing happens. I have over the years discovered that the worst thing that could realistically happen is usually not as scary as the nightmare my fear-fueled mind could produce. Finding clarity in this way doesn't take much time or effort and it can help you to avoid mind made suffering. And help you to get going, step outside of your comfort zone and take that chance.

**Add value and positivity to someone else's life.** What you send out you tend to get back from the world and the people in it. As I stated earlier, not from everyone. And not every time. But what you send out there matters a whole lot. What you give them and how you treat them is what you'll get back. And the way you treat others and how you think of them also tend to have a big effect on how you treat and think about yourself. So, give value and spread the positivity by (examples):

- **Helping out.** Doing something to help someone else usually produces a strong sense of happiness and fulfillment.
- **Just listening.** Sometimes people don't want any direct help. They just want someone to be there listening as they vent.
- **Boosting the mood.** Smile. Give hugs. Play uplifting music when hanging out with a friend or suggest an inspiring movie for your movie night. Or encourage when someone has had a bad day or are going through a tough time.

**Learn to take criticism in a healthy way.** One of the most common fears is the fear of criticism. It can hold people back from doing what they want in life. Because having negativity flowing out of someone's mouth or email and it being about you can hurt. And being rejected can hurt. But if you want to act on what you deep down want then criticism is unavoidable. So, the key is learning to manage it in a healthier way. By doing so your fear of it will lessen and it will hurt less if you do get criticized.

**Start your day in a positive way.** How you start your day usually sets the tone for the rest of your day. So be careful about how you spend your mornings. If you get going at full speed, lost in future troubles in your mind then the stress, perceived loss of power of over your life and negative thoughts will ramp up quickly. If you on the other hand start your day by moving slowly, by having an uplifting conversation with your family or friend or you spend some time with reading or listening to inspiring and helpful articles or podcasts over breakfast or during your ride to work then that can make a big difference for how your whole day will go.

**Mindfully move through your day.** When you spend your time in the present moment then it becomes so much easier to access positive emotions and to stay practical about what you can actually do about something in your life. When you get lost in the past or future like so many of us have spent a lot of time on doing then worries very easily become bigger. And failures and mistakes from the past being replayed over and over in your mind drag you down into pessimism. By moving slowly through your morning and hopefully through much of the rest of your day it becomes easier to mindfully stay in the moment you are in.

Another simple way to reconnect with the moment you are in, and to put your full attention there again, is to focus just on what is going on around you right now for a minute. See it. Hear it. Smell it. Feel the sun, rain, or cold wind on your skin. It might sound like a small and insignificant thing to do. But this simplifying reconnection with the moment can have an incredibly positive effect on the rest of your day.

Sharing just a few of my life experiences in this book, and often on social media, has been therapeutic in a lot of ways for me. It helped to release and unhinge dormant situations that have haunted me daily simply because I held on to them. You can unknowingly hold demons hostage for many years. Crazy huh? Equally important, I have become transparent during my transformation, and if any of this can help anyone, or at least one, then, I have accomplished a small goal. Everyone has a story to tell and because we're all unique individuals with different ideas, thoughts, and visions, we may take various ways to reach our destination. We want to walk our journey in peace. I am not an expert with any of this I've shared, but it comes from my heart intimately. Men do not usually say to themselves or anyone that they love themselves.

Well, my friends, if I may be the first to write it out and say it aloud, "Anthony Jameyson Smith LOVES HIMSELF BECAUSE HE LEARNED HOW TO BE HAPPY."

# References

- www.chopra.com
- www.psychologytoday.com
- www.forbes.com
- www.elitedaily.com
- www.psychalive.com

# Journal

# Journal

# Journal